1 MONTH OF
FREE
READING

at

www.ForgottenBooks.com

By purchasing this book you are
eligible for one month membership to
ForgottenBooks.com, giving you
unlimited access to our entire
collection of over 1,000,000 titles via
our web site and mobile apps.

To claim your free month visit:

www.forgottenbooks.com/free979609

ISBN 978-0-260-87711-6
PIBN 10979609

This book is a reproduction of an important historical work. Forgotten Books uses
state-of-the-art technology to digitally reconstruct the work, preserving the original format
whilst repairing imperfections present in the aged copy. In rare cases, an imperfection in
the original, such as a blemish or missing page, may be replicated in our edition. We do,
however, repair the vast majority of imperfections successfully; any imperfections that
remain are intentionally left to preserve the state of such historical works.

ιe

2 F

Foreign

CROPS AND MARKETS

VOLUME 64   NUMBER 12

HOGS (Page 234)   TOBACCO (Page 241)

DAIRY PRODUCTS (Page 237)

CONTENTS

FOR RELEASE

MONDAY

MARCH 24, 1952

UNITED STATES DEPARTMENT OF AGRICULTURE
OFFICE OF FOREIGN AGRICULTURAL RELATIONS
WASHINGTON 25, D.C.

L A T E   N E W S

The Government of India has abolished the export duty on peanut oil, kardi seed (safflower seed) and niger seed in order to maintain or improve exports and foreign exchange earnings.

- - -

Imports of cotton into the United States during January 1952 amounted to 15,450 bales (of 500 pounds gross), making an August-January total of 25,544 bales. All except 1,000 bales of the January imports were received from Mexico, nearly completing the 1951-52 import quota from that country. Total imports of 25,544 bales during August-January 1951-52 include 17,302 bales from Mexico, 4,202 from India, and 3,876 from Peru.

- - - -

The Government of Pakistan has established (about March 15) minimum prices for cotton as follows, in equivalent U.S. cents a pound: 289F Sind, SG, Fine, 33.73 cents; 4F Punjab, SG, Fine, 32.27 cents; 289F Punjab, SG, Fine, 35.20 cents. These figures apparently do not include the export tax of 13.85 cents a pound.

- - - -

The Government of India announced on March 16, 1952, a 50 percent reduction in the export tax on cotton from 400 to 200 rupees per bale (equivalent to a reduction from about 21.27 U.S. cents a pound to 10.64 cents). This reduction was reportedly made in an effort to stimulate exports of certain types of Indian cotton which are in excessive supply. Total supply this year is greatly improved due to increased domestic production and large imports during the current season.

- - - -

A Venezuelan Government official has announced that the plan for increased domestic production of cotton in the 1951-52 season has been successful. Production was increased from 5,000 bales in 1950-51 to 18,000

(Continued on Page 257)

FOREIGN CROPS AND MARKETS

Published weekly to inform producers, processors, distributors and consumers of farm products of current developments abroad in the crop and livestock industries, foreign trends in prices and consumption of farm products, and world agricultural trade. Circulation of this peri- odical is free to those persons in the U. S. needing the information it contains in farming, business and professional operations. Issued by the Office of Foreign Agricultural Relations of the U. S. Department of Agriculture, Washington 25, D. C.

WORLD HOG NUMBERS IN 1951 AND 1952 1/

World hog numbers on January 1, 1952, were estimated by the Office of Foreign Agricultural Relations at 305 million head, a record total. This is an increase of around 3 percent from a year earlier when over 296 million were on farms. World numbers are now 5 percent above the 1936-40 average with the gain largely in North and South America. In Europe, numbers are close to the prewar level with the increases in Western European countries nearly offsetting declines in the East.

The rate of increase for the past year of 3 percent is about one-half that for the previous 3 years indicating a slowing-up in the postwar expansion in hog numbers. With consumer demand for meats somewhat more nearly met in important countries and hog prices less attractive to producers in relation to feed prices, hog numbers a year hence are likely to be no higher than at the beginning of 1952.

Hog numbers in the United States were reported on January 1, 1952, to be up 2 percent or approximately 1 million head above the previous year. Hogs under 6 months increased, reflecting the larger pig crop in the fall of 1951. The number of sows and gilts were down around 8 percent indicating a decrease in breeding intentions. The outlook for a decline is generally attributed to a less favorable relationship of hog prices to corn prices.

Canadian hog numbers increased sharply during 1951 and were estimated at the end of the year to be slightly under 6.5 million head compared with 5.4 million a year earlier. The large feed crop, strong market demand and good prices greatly stimulated breeding operations. Hog numbers in Canada advanced to an all time high during the war years and then declined, but, since 1948, numbers have steadily increased. Because of the depressing affect of foot-and-mouth disease on the Canadian livestock market the future hog trend is obscured. Nevertheless, due to the extremely favorable feed position, Canadian breeders will not necessarily follow United States farmers in reducing inventories. Hog numbers are expected to be at least maintained close to present levels.

In Argentina, hog numbers were reduced during the 1949-50 drought and conditions had not been satisfactory for recovery by mid-1951. Prices were temporarily very profitable to producers due to the beef shortage and small export contracts, but the feed outlook was doubtful and there has been no steady market for output in excess of adequate domestic needs.

Hog numbers in Europe have steadily increased during postwar years because of intensive breeding and feeding programs and the generally satisfactory feed and forage supplies in important producing areas. Demand for pork and pork products has been good. Encouraged by firm prices, European farmers have expanded operations. In 1951, however, Denmark, The Netherlands and Austria reduced their hog populations as high prices for imported feed

1/ A more extensive statement will soon be available as a Foreign Agriculture Circular published by the Office of Foreign Agricultural Relations, U. S. Department of Agriculture, Washington 25, D. C.

HOGS: Number in specified countries, averages 1936-40 and 1941-45, annual 1947-1952

Continent and country	Month of estimate 1/	Average 1936-40 (Thousands)	1941-45 (Thousands)	1947 (Thousands)	1948 (Thousands)	1949 (Thousands)	1950 (Thousands)	1951 2/ (Thousands)	1952 2/ (Thousands)
NORTH AMERICA									
Canada 1/	Dec. 1 1/	4,078	7,472	5,459	5,381	4,604	5,413	5,419	6,498
El Salvador	July	559	460	283	348	-	-	350	-
Guatemala	July	213	2/ 274	-	1/ 374	-	4/ 413	1/ -	-
Honduras	July	235	2/ 247	323	399	372	407	-	-
Mexico	Dec. 1 1/	2/3/ 4,965	3/ 5,212	5,314	-	5,600	5,600	6,000	-
Nicaragua		3/ 250	9/ 225	-	250	-	250	-	250
United States	Jan. 1	48,352	66,391	56,810	54,590	56,257	58,852	62,852	63,903
Cuba	Dec.31 1/	3/ 904	3/ 825	-	1,700	1,800	1,800	1,800	-
Estimated total		61,400	83,100	72,700	70,800	72,000	75,600	80,000	82,000
EUROPE									
Austria	Dec. 1 1/	2/ 2,849	1,915	1,490	1,724	1,618	1/ 1,927	2/ 2,523	2,448
Belgium	Jan. 1 1/	1/ 1,005	545	7/ 776	648	912	1,361	1,234	1,360
Bulgaria	Dec.31 1/	2/ 875	912	7/ 870	825	-	-	-	-
Czechoslovakia	Jan. 1	3,174	3,025	2,944	2,566	3,242	3,120	3,616	3,229
Denmark	Jan.	2,997	1,919	1/ 1,687	1/ 1,604	1/ 1,944	-	-	-
Finland	Mar. 1	8/ 435	266	335	304	409	468	1/ 440	-
France	Fall	7,034	7/ 4,738	7/ 5,335	7/ 5,678	7/ 6,424	7/ 6,747	7/ 6,824	7,101
Germany-Western	Dec.31 1/	12,660	7/ 9,390	7/ 6,429	7/ 5,516	7/ 6,755	7/ 9,698	7/ 11,890	13,583
Greece	Dec.31 1/	3/ 532	-	490	480	509	530	570	590
Hungary	Spring	3,620	3,554	2,119	2,350	3,250	-	-	-
Ireland	June	978	505	457	457	675	645	558	-
Italy	July	6/ 3,750	3,380	3,500	3,891	3,949	4,375	4,025	4,370
Luxembourg	Dec. 1 1/	148	92	95	100	106	110	100	95
Netherlands	Dec. 1 1/	1,725	3/ 860	1,062	937	1,158	1,795	2,273	2,110
Norway	June 20	393	210	259	248	419	422	386	-
Poland	June 30	6/ 9,684	6/ 1,253	-	-	-	-	-	-
Portugal	Dec.31 1/	6/ 1,206	-	-	1,200	-	-	-	-
Rumania	Dec.31 1/	2/ 2,640	-	1,384	1,459	-	-	-	-
Spain	Dec.31 1/	6/ 4,944	2/ 5,146	-	-	5,568	-	-	5,575
Sweden	Summer	1,292	934	1,189	1,195	1,238	1,278	1,346	1,379
Switzerland	April	915	672	710	767	877	908	892	950
United Kingdom	June	4,380	2,110	1,628	2,151	2,823	2,986	3,891	-
Yugoslavia	Dec.31 1/	3,238	-	-	-	-	-	-	-
Estimated total		76,600	54,800	49,200	51,000	58,900	68,000	72,300	75,700
U.S.S.R. (Europe and Asia)	Jan. 1	6/ 32,300	-	8,600	12,000	15,000	19,000	24,100	26,700

	Date								
ASIA									
British Malaya	Dec.31 1/	746	3/ 380	361	444	452	475	-	-
Burma 2/	May	538	-	309	402	-	-	-	-
China 9/	Jan.1	6/ 63,000	58,000	59,000	-	-	-	3,700	3,800
India	Dec.31 1/	2,777	6/ 3,665	-	-	-	716	560	-
Japan	Mar.31	960	427	906	1,167	1,362	-	-	-
Formosa	Dec.31 1/	1,669	1,043	300	521	545	-	-	-
Korea-South	Dec.31 1/	828	515	1,143	-	-	1,234	1,350	-
Indonesia	Dec.31 1/	1,199	-	-	-	3,533	3,899	4,159	-
Philippine Republic	Jan.1	4,398	-	1,143	-	-	-	-	4,500
Estimated total		83,900	76,100	74,500	74,900	76,200	77,600	77,700	78,000
SOUTH AMERICA									
Argentina	July	3/ 3,674	6,860	10/ 2,955	2,500	3,000	2,600	2,800	2,90
Brazil		3/ 23,224	3/ 24,672	1/ 23,680	24,500	24,500	1/ 25,000	1/ 26,059	-
Chile	June	3/ 420	3/ 405	-	572	600	600	660	-
Colombia	Dec.31 1/	3/ 1,572	3/ 1,659	1,679	2,059	2,162	2,470	2,782	-
Ecuador		3/ 350	3/ 853	1,000	1,140	-	-	-	-
Peru		800	3/ 657	-	777	-	-	975	-
Uruguay	May	3/ 373	3/ 354	1/ 250	250	-	-	270	-
Estimated total		31,300	36,900	32,500	33,400	34,200	34,700	36,500	36,600
AFRICA									
Algeria	April	58	136	203	142	160	137	200	-
Nyasaland 12/	Dec.31 1/	65	49	-	-	80	91	52	-
French 12/	Dec.31 1/	64	123	-	68	97	103	84	-
Madagascar 12/	Dec.31 1/	578	523	396	410	400	420	399	-
Mozambique	Dec.31 1/	70	59	57	60	68	82	85	-
Northern Rhodesia	Dec.31 1/	29	34	55	58	43	47	-	-
Angola		6/ 410	6/ 484	-	400	-	-	-	-
Southern Rhodesia	Dec.31 1/	115	148	143	117	103	107	98	-
Tunisia	Dec.31 1/	24	22	31	42	42	28	-	-
Union of South Africa	August	3/ 1,007	6/ 1,174	1,150	1,300	1,400	1,450	-	-
Estimated total		3,400	3,800	3,800	4,000	4,100	4,200	4,200	4,100
OCEANIA									
Australia	Mar.31	1/ 1,242	1,643	1,273	1,255	1,196	1,123	1,133	1,125
New Zealand	Jan.31	753	643	546	548	545	552	-	-
Estimated total		2,100	2,500	2,000	2,000	1,900	1,900	1,800	1,900
Estimated world total		291,000	273,200	243,300	248,100	262,300	281,000	296,600	305,000

1/ End of year estimates (October to December) included under following year for comparisons and totals. Thus for Canada the December 1946 estimate of 5,459,000 head is shown under 1947. 2/ Preliminary. 3/ Averages for 2 to 4 years only. 4/ Agricultural Census of 1950. 5/ June 6/ Census or estimate for single year. 7/ Official statistics may be an under-estimate of actual numbers. 8/ September. 9/ Includes China Proper (22 provinces), Manchuria, Jehol and Sinkiang (Turkestan). 10/ Census May 10-12, 1947. 11/ Year 1934. 12/ Number taxed only.

Office of Foreign Agricultural Relations. Prepared or estimated on the basis of official statistics of foreign governments, reports of United States Foreign Service officers, and other information. Data for countries having changed boundaries relate to present territory, unless otherwise noted. Totals include estimates for countries for which official statistics are unavailable.

made hog raising less attractive. With the exception of Austria, the latest estimates bring these countries more in line with prewar averages. The leveling or partial curtailment of hog numbers in many other European countries is anticipated during the coming year.

In Western Germany, hogs increased sharply to reach a population above the 1936-40 average. Increases are associated with good prices and adequate feed stocks, but reduction in numbers during 1952 is likely. Only a repetition of the abnormal 1951 marketing situation where consumers demande pork at any price or a marked improvement in the feed position could change the outlook. France increased hogs slightly and numbers are now on a par with the prewar level. Numbers in Spain were reported close to the 1949 level, but above the 1936-40 average.

The sharp upward trend in hog numbers continued in the United Kingdom during 1951, but because of feed difficulties no increase in 1952 is expected.

The Soviet Union continued to expand breeding operations during 1951. Hog numbers were estimated in early 1952 at around 11 percent above a year earlier, a substantial increase, but still below prewar. Good supplies of feed during recent years undoubtedly contributed to stimulate the increase.

Hog numbers in Australia have changed very little in postwar years. Production may be moderately lower during 1952, however, due to shorter supplies of skim milk, the leading protein feed, and higher prices for feed wheat, corn and grain sorghum.

This is one of a series of regularly scheduled reports on world agricultural production approved by the Office of Foreign Agricultural Relations Committee on Foreign Crops and Livestock Statistics. It is based in part upon U. S. Foreign Service reports.

WORLD PRODUCTION OF DAIRY PRODUCTS, FOURTH QUARTER AND ANNUAL, 1951 [1]/

Fourth Quarter:

Over-all production of manufactured dairy products in many of the principal producing countries of the world in the fourth quarter of 1951 declined below comparable 1950, according to information available to the Office of Foreign Agricultural Relations. Butter, canned milk and dried milk production decreased markedly in this period, while cheese output dropped only slightly below the level of a year ago.

Varying factors contributed to a decline in milk production in several countries, which in turn affected the output of dairy products by limiting the quantity of milk available for utilization in manufacturing. In Australia, where the important dairying States of Queensland

[1]/ A more extensive statement will soon be published as a Foreign Agriculture Circular available from the Office of Foreign Agricultural Relations , U.S. Department of Agriculture, Washington 25, D. C.

and New South Wales had not recovered from the devastating drought and
bush fires which ruined pastures and depleted herds, milk production
was greatly curtailed. Pastures in Argentina were very dry early in
the quarter, resulting in lower milk output than in the same period
last year.

An outbreak of foot-and-mouth disease affected milk production
in Denmark and to some extent in the Netherlands. Lower output in Sweden
was attributed to the reduced profitability of milk production due to
higher feed costs. A drop in cow numbers in the United Kingdom as a
result of the relatively unfavorable controlled milk prices caused a
decline in milk production in this quarter.

Dairying countries in which milk production was maintained at or
slightly exceeded last year's level were New Zealand, the Netherlands,
Switzerland, Canada and the United States.

Butter production in the final quarter of 1951 was 6 percent below
the same quarter of 1950 and showed the greatest decline of any dairy
product. Production declined in Australia, Argentina, Denmark, the
Netherlands, Sweden, the United Kingdom, Ireland and the United States
and more than offset increases in New Zealand, the Union of South
Africa, Switzerland, Western Germany and Canada.

Cheese production in the fourth quarter of 1951 was only slightly
below the same quarter a year earlier. A marked increase in output in
Argentina resulted from the marked diversion of the decreased milk supply
from butter to cheese wherever possible. Production in Denmark and the
Netherlands and Switzerland increased somewhat, due to diversion of milk
from butter to cheese in Denmark and the Netherlands and due to a
larger milk supply in the Netherlands and Switzerland.

In Australia, decreased production of cheese reflected the unfavorable milk producing conditions that continued into the fourth
quarter, while in New Zealand, the lower output was due to the
diversion of milk supplies to butter and casein. With less milk available
for cheese manufacture in the United Kingdom, Canada and the United States,
production dropped below that of a year ago.

Total canned milk production decreased approximately 9 percent in
the 5 major producing countries in the fourth quarter of 1951, compared
with the preceding year, although moderate gains were reported in
Australia, the Netherlands and Canada. Output was down slightly in
the United Kingdom and in the United States, which accounts for about 80
percent of the total, output was down 12 percent.

Dried milk production in the October-December quarter was 12 percent
below the corresponding period of 1950. Output in the Netherlands and
Canada rose in the fourth quarter but not enough to offset the marked
declines in Australia, Sweden, the United Kingdom and the United States.

Prospects for dairy production in the Southern Hemisphere in the
early months of 1952 are considered good only in New Zealand, where
conditions continue to be favorable. In the Union of South Africa,

(Continued on Page 255)

DAIRY PRODUCTS: Output in principal producing and exporting countries,
4th quarter (calendar) 1951, with comparisons

Country and product	Average 1934-38 1,000 pounds	Total 1950 1,000 pounds	Total 1951 1,000 pounds	1950 4th quarter 1,000 pounds	1951 1st quarter 1,000 pounds	1951 2nd quarter 1,000 pounds	1951 3rd quarter 1,000 pounds	1951 4th quarter 1,000 pounds	Fourth Quarter 1951/1950 Percent
Butter									
Canada	1/ 254,774	2/ 261,464	257,604	2/ 44,358	25,365	84,815	99,875	47,549	107
United States	1,673,328	2/ 1,386,290	1,214,685	2/ 242,692	2/ 260,235	379,315	2/ 349,860	2/ 225,275	93
Belgium	46,179	2/3/ 71,250	—	14,506	11,918	22,433	24,350	—	88
Denmark	400,660	394,623	372,577	87,963	81,191	112,655	101,191	77,602	88
France	4/5/444,888	496,000	—	—	—	—	—	—	—
Germany, Western	6/ 360,000	2/ 570,551	7/ 610,000	131,785	116,570	171,611	179,783	2/ 142,036	108
Ireland	89,400	82,672	7/ 70,000	13,448	3,326	22,444	32,425	2/ 11,805	88
Netherlands	201,000	205,497	180,644	38,150	32,041	2/ 61,998	56,167	2/ 30,438	80
Norway	24,930	25,472	—	3,293	4,630	9,279	7,685	—	—
Sweden	151,109	2/ 239,356	234,349	50,082	49,901	67,965	70,988	45,495	91
Switzerland 4/	57,760	2/ 42,549	55,115	2/ 9,482	9,034	12,308	17,285	16,478	174
United Kingdom	44,200	36,601	7/ 11,700	2,284	3,181	4,077	3,136	1,306	57
Argentina	65,742	2/ 99,769	82,452	2/ 33,016	2/ 26,235	24,251	8,818	2/ 23,148	70
Union of South Africa	27,725	2/ 99,715	65,973	16,089	21,974	14,688	12,049	17,262	76
Australia	8/ 437,032	2/ 378,882	314,376	2/ 138,589	99,964	47,461	62,032	104,919	105
New Zealand - total	9/ 366,049	2/ 372,515	410,025	2/ 165,984	124,481	38,248	73,472	173,824	105
Export gradings	10/314,753	309,682	7/ 352,100	138,184	119,439	30,618	54,089	7/ 147,954	107
Cheese									
Canada	119,924	2/ 97,654	85,260	2/ 15,423	2/ 5,010	27,197	38,424	2/ 14,629	95
United States	643,234	2/1,192,557	1,157,560	217,172	2/ 235,250	379,510	2/ 330,125	2/ 212,675	98
Denmark	68,820	129,630	165,345	29,761	34,833	52,469	46,516	31,527	106
France	4/5/363,098	562,173	—	—	—	—	—	—	—
Italy 11/	523,518	2/ 524,695	—	—	—	—	—	—	—
Netherlands	200,000	235,511	299,192	45,488	2/ 37,839	87,494	86,390	2/ 47,469	104
Norway	39,067	56,175	—	8,982	2/ 13,354	21,895	18,362	—	—
Sweden	71,269	2/ 113,574	120,007	21,016	29,441	35,902	34,171	20,493	98
Switzerland	111,729	2/ 124,119	116,844	2/ 31,571	12,926	31,089	39,220	33,609	106
United Kingdom 4/	109,000	123,873	7/ 97,250	12,768	24,282	34,496	30,240	2/ 8,232	64
Argentina	67,873	2/ 215,092	209,437	2/ 65,496	2/ 59,083	52,911	15,873	2/ 81,570	124
Union of South Africa	10,195	20,567	21,088	2/ 6,252	6,885	4,339	4,171	5,693	91
Australia	8/ 49,111	2/ 103,689	93,228	2/ 45,772	22,149	9,905	22,010	39,164	86
New Zealand - total	2/ 201,272	2/ 238,469	227,945	2/ 103,264	76,821	26,396	32,704	92,064	89
Export gradings	10/194,175	224,395	7/ 223,500	93,054	81,570	38,221	17,881	7/ 85,828	92

Canned milk 12/									Ratio
Canada 13/	104,335	287,798	327,844	49,623	44,029	120,531	110,213	53,071	107
United States 12/	2,469,535	3,992,880	3,972,115	729,510	855,450	1,396,225	1,084,025	636,415	87
Cuba 5/	32,564	49,728	12,390	—	—	—	—	—	—
Denmark	4,95	94,990	—	—	—	—	—	—	—
France 13/	28,953	94,798	—	—	—	—	—	—	106
Netherlands	304,896	379,506	393,202	85,847	8,726	116,341	98,180	90,955	106
Switzerland	14,198	—	—	—	—	—	—	—	—
United Kingdom 17/	378,560	297,740	18,750	18,995	30,823	97,216	32,973	17,738	93
Argentina	—	16,786	—	—	—	—	—	—	—
Australia 8/	43,894	146,273	146,603	56,491	35,279	20,418	30,989	59,917	106
New Zealand 12/	11,273	—	—	—	—	—	—	—	—

Dried milk 14/									Ratio
Canada 11/	26,079	67,593	69,409	11,847	7,710	22,664	25,146	13,889	117
United States 12/	203,555	972,671	825,625	136,536	177,145	314,180	220,950	113,350	83
Belgium	5,500	9,459	—	1,170	936	7,271	7,018	—	—
Denmark	2,205	24,82	—	—	—	—	—	—	—
France 13/	7,685	15,432	73,992	5,655	7,379	30,806	27,039	8,768	155
Netherlands	56,638	91,134	17,756	4,252	5,691	5,178	4,850	2,077	48
Sweden	1,351	19,890	—	—	—	—	—	—	—
Switzerland	2,381	—	—	—	—	—	—	—	—
United Kingdom 17/	33,600	77,952	50,000	5,287	7,437	27,298	11,917	3,408	64
Argentina 8/	16,971	12,454	—	—	—	—	—	—	96
Australia 18/	17,429	92,401	85,307	35,386	19,344	11,525	20,496	33,942	96

1/ Average 1935-39. 2/ Revised. 3/ Total production is estimated at 162,807,000 pounds in 1950. 4/ Total production. 5/ Less than a 5-year average. 6/ Average 1935-38. 7/ Estimated. 8/ Production year beginning July 1. 9/ Production year beginning April 1. 10/ Mark beginning August 1. 11/ Total cheese, and includes cheese made from the milk of sheep and goats. 12/ Both bulk and case goods. 13/ For 1937. 14/ Total dried-whole and dried-skin milk for human use. 15/ Quantity small. 16/ Includes infants' food, health beverages, &c. 17/ Production of dried-whole and dried-skin milk was ... qts in 1950 and 57,016,000 qts in 1951. 18/ For 1938.

Office of Foreign Agricultural Relations a. Prepared or had from official statistics, U. S. Foreign Service reports, and other March 24, B.

WORLD FLUE-CURED TOBACCO PRODUCTION AT NEW RECORD LEVEL

The estimated world flue-cured tobacco production of 2,377 million pounds during the fiscal year July 1951-June 1952 surpasses the preceding year's record level of 1,988 million pounds by 20 percent and the 1949-50 output of 1,811 million pounds by 31 percent. Substantial increases in output occurred in many of the important producing countries and especially in the United States, China, Southern Rhodesia, and Canada. Decreases were recorded for Brazil, the Union of South Africa, India, Pakistan, and New Zealand.

Increased world demand for flue-cured leaf, used mostly in the manufacture of Virginia-type and United States blended cigarettes, has resulted in a progressive increase in output of this type of tobacco. Consumers in practically all countries are shifting from products containing dark and cigar tobacco to flue-cured and other light types used principally in cigarettes. Effective world demand for flue-cured loaf, especially United States flue-cured, would probably be substantially larger if it were not for restrictions by many countries on the use of foreign exchange for the import of tobacco.

United States. The 1951 flue-cured crop was 14 percent above the latest estimate for 1950 and 29 percent above 1949. The estimated 1951 production is 1,434 million pounds from 1,110,000 acres. This compares with 1,257 million pounds from 958,400 acres in 1950 and 1,115 million pounds from 935,400 acres in 1949. Increased acreage planted to flue-cured leaf was responsible for increased production, as the 1951 yield per acre was slightly less than the 1950 yield. The United States crop represented 60 percent of the estimated world production of flue-cured tobacco in 1951. This compares with 63 percent in 1950, 62 percent in 1949, and a prewar annual average of 70 percent.

Canada. Flue-cured production in Canada in 1951 is estimated at 141.6 million pounds, an all-time record. It was 31 percent above the 1950 output of 108.2 million pounds, and 21 percent above the 116.7 million pounds, the previous record crop produced in 1949. A larger acreage as well as increase in yield per acre were responsible for the higher 1951 production. The yield per acre for 1951 is estimated at 1,276 pounds, a near record yield, as compared with 1,175 pounds in 1950 and 1,286 pounds, an all-time record yield, in 1949.

China. China's 1951 flue-cured harvest (excluding Manchuria) is estimated at 260 million pounds from 297,000 acres as compared with only 80 million pounds from 81,000 acres in 1950.

India. Flue-cured production in India decreased from 104.5 million pounds, a revised estimate for 1950-51, to 95.0 million pounds in 1951-52. This is a decrease of 9 percent, and is attributed to adverse weather conditions during the growing season. Information regarding acreages shows increases in both 1950-51 and 1951-52.

FLUE-CURED TOBACCO: World acreage and production, 1951 with comparisons 1/

Country	Acreage				Production			
	Average 1935-39	1949	1950	1951 2/	Average 1935-39	1949	1950	1951 2/
	Acres	Acres	Acres	Acres	1,000 pounds	1,000 pounds	1,000 pounds	1,000 pounds
Canada	50,703	90,733	92,080	111,020	54,616	116,568	108,202	141,625
Mexico	3/	3/	3/	3/	800 4/	4,630	3,750	3,858
United States	981,400	935,400	958,400	1,110,100	863,620	1,114,508	1,257,280	1,433,650
Italy	3/	8,157	9,214	10,353	2,846	14,775	19,460	21,164
China	132,800	3/	80,723	297,000	150,900	3/	90,000	260,000
Pakistan	10,510	1,600	3/	3/	13,930	1,308	4,165	4,000
India	67,000 4/	150	5,500	4,500	31,280	95,400	104,500	95,000
Japan	40,830	51,346	64,665	72,911	62,350	67,608	105,600	108,704
Taiwan (Formosa)	1,988	16,595	12,444	14,245	3,235	18,982	12,278	17,196
Korea	7,674	13,118	16,233	56,900	11,839	22,146	21,600	16,535
Thailand (Siam)	3/	33,620	45,600	12,385	3/	9,920	13,974	13,228
Argentina	955 4/	6,425	12,355	3/	918	6,173	11,023	3/
Brazil	3/	32,247	32,123	33,606	3/	43,375	44,974	33,069
Nyasaland	3/	5,000	3/	3/	2,574	2,604	4,010	4,000
Northern Rhodesia	3/	15,500	3/	3/	3/	7,000	10,149	14,000
Southern Rhodesia	48,010	152,717	172,000	192,000	24,623	105,492	87,500	110,000
Union of South Africa	3/	32,201	3/	3/	4,996	22,108	21,442	17,800
Australia	9,913	4,561	6,628	7,678	5,276	4,138	4,250	6,450
New Zealand	1,740	3,899	3,950	3,666	1,370	4,700	5,500	5,000
All other countries 6/	37,170	215,015	316,482	235,565	2,682	149,654	68,070	71,313
Estimated World Total	1,390,723	1,768,134	1,828,397	2,261,529	1,237,855	1,811,189	1,987,727	2,376,592

1/ Year beginning July 1. For north temperate zone countries, harvests July through [...] or of the year shown; for all other countries, harvests January through [...] of the following year. 2/ Preliminary. 3/ Data not available. 4/ Less than a 5-year average. 5/ No flue-cured production in prewar years. 6/ Includes approximations for countries not listed, and where data not available.

Office of Foreign Agricultural Relations. Official estimates of foreign countries, reports from U. S. Foreign Service Officers, results of office research and other information.

Japan. Japan's 1951 flue-cured production is estimated at 108.7 million pounds from 72,911 acres. This is slightly higher than the 1950 output of 105.6 million pounds from 64,665 acres, and much higher than the 67.6 million pounds from 51,346 acres produced in 1949.

Other Far Eastern Countries. Total flue-cured production in Korea, Thailand (Siam), Pakistan, Taiwan, (Formosa) and Manchuria is estimated at 48.7 million pounds as compared with 67.0 million pounds produced in those countries in 1950-51. For other Far Eastern countries where production is limited the 1951-52 output is estimated above the 1950-51 and 1949-50 harvests.

Southern Rhodesia. Flue-cured leaf production in 1951-52 is unofficially estimated at 110 million pounds from 192,000 acres. This is a substantial increase over the 87.5 million pounds from 172,000 acres produced in 1950-51. It is reported that the quality of this season's leaf will be below average due to excessive rainfall during the growing season. Heavy rains also lowered the production from early season expectations and some observers report that there may be further reduction in output before the crop is harvested and cured.

Other Countries. The Union of South Africa's 1951-52 production is placed at only 17.8 million pounds as compared with 21.4 million pounds in 1950-51. The decrease results from drought conditions during the current growing season. The remaining important African flue-cured producing countries, namely, Northern Rhodesia and Nyasaland, report larger 1951-52 harvests. Brazil's 1951-52 flue-cured production is estimated at 33.1 million pounds as compared with nearly 45.0 million pounds in 1950-51. The decrease is attributed to lower yields per acre due to unfavorable growing conditions during the season. Other countries producing flue-cured leaf, and for which changes in production from 1950-51 were limited, include Argentina, Mexico, El Salvador, Nicaragua, Italy, Spain, British East Africa, New Zealand, and Australia.

This is one of a series of regularly scheduled reports of world agricultural production approved by the Office of Foreign Agricultural Relations Committee on Foreign Crop and Livestock Statistics. It is based in part upon U.S. Foreign Service reports.

COMMODITY DEVELOPMENTS

TOBACCO

CANADA'S TOBACCO
EXPORTS HIGHER

Canada's exports of unmanufactured tobacco during 1951 were 30 percent above 1950 and 86 percent above 1949, according to official export statistics released by the Canadian Government.

The country's leaf exports during the 1951 calendar year totaled 29.2 million pounds as compared with 22.5 million pounds in 1950 and 15.7 million pounds in 1949. Flue-cured leaf, the most important export type, comprised 28.3 million pounds, or 97 percent of the total 1951 unmanufactured tobacco exports. This compares with 19.7 million pounds, or 87 percent in 1950 and 14.0 million, or 89 percent in 1949. The remaining 1951 exports consisted of 597,000 pounds of Burley, 201,000 pounds of dark leaf and 72,000 pounds of other types of leaf. In addition to leaf tobacco, Canada exported 241,900 pounds of stems and cuttings during 1951. During 1950, shipments of stems and cuttings totaled 4.3 million pounds.

The United Kingdom, the most important 1951 export outlet, took 23.2 million pounds, or 79 percent of all leaf exports. Flue-cured leaf comprised 22.6 million pounds, or 97 percent of the exports to the United Kingdom. During 1950, the United Kingdom took 15.0 million pounds, or 63 percent of total leaf exports. Australia, the second most important 1951 outlet, took 1.9 million pounds, all of which was flue-cured type.

CANADA: Exports of leaf tobacco by types, 1951 with comparisons

Type of leaf	1949	1950	1951
	1,000 pounds	1,000 pounds	1,000 pounds
Flue-cured	14,018	19,670	28,310
Burley	1,380	893	597
Dark	251	185	201
Other	76	1,760	72
Total 1/	15,725	22,508	29,180

1/ Does not include stems and cuttings.

Dominican Bureau of Statistics.

Canada's 1951 exports of cigarettes totaled 36.3 million pieces as compared with only 9.1 million during 1950. French Africa, the most important cigarette export outlet during 1951, took 19.9 million pieces, or 55 percent of the total. Japan, the second most important outlet, took 8.5 million, or 23 percent; the United States ranked third, with 5.7 million, or 16 percent; and Greenland, fourth, with 1.5 million, or 4 percent. The remaining 0.7 million cigarettes were taken in relatively small quantities by numerous countries including the United Kingdom, Bermuda, Argentina, Chile, Columbia, Peru, France, the Netherlands, Korea, and Japan.

FATS AND OILS

FIJI ISLANDS COPRA PRODUCTION
AND EXPORTS INCREASE IN 1951

Production of copra in Fiji during 1951 is estimated by the trade at about 30,000 long tons as against the official 1950 figure of 28,197 tons, reports Philip E. Haring, American Consulate, Noumea.

The Fiji Department of Agriculture's program for the planting and rehabilitation of coconut plantations, sponsored by the Fijian Affairs Board, did not fulfill its ambitious project for planting 15,000 acres of new trees during 1951, but it did make visible progress. Some 151,000 selected seed-nuts, sufficient to plant 3,024 acres, have been started in nurseries, and 1,064 acres have been

planted from the nurseries. The Fijian Affairs Board is working with
the Fiji Department of Agriculture in these programs, as native
Fijians, working on communally-owned lands, account for from 50 to 60
percent of the Colony's copra production.

Under the terms of a 9-year contract concluded between Fiji and
the British Ministry of Food on January 1, 1949, all of the Colony's
exportable surplus of coconut products is at the disposal of the
United Kingdom which establishes fixed buying prices at the first of
each year. During 1950 and January-November 1951 exports were as
follows (in long tons):

	1950	January-November 1951
Copra	10,158	11,286
Coconut oil	10,083	10,470
Coconut meal	5,009	4,571

Although December 1951 figures are not available, exports of copra
and coconut oil for the 11 months were above the tonnages for both
products in 1950. As in the previous year, coconut oil was the third
most important export by value in 1951, and copra again remained in
fourth place.

Prices paid by the British Ministry of Food during 1951 increased
by about 10 percent from those paid in 1950 and were as follows:

Copra (Fair Merchantable Sundried Quality) - £53-15 per long
     ton, f.o.b. ($150.50)
Coconut oil - £88 per long ton, f.o.b. ($246.40)
Coconut meal - £15 per long ton, f.o.b. ($42)

In December 1951, the Fiji Copra Board accepted the proposals of the
Ministry of Food for a 10 percent increase in the price the latter
would pay for copra in 1952. This amount is the maximum yearly price
rise permitted under the contract, and would increase the buying price
of copra to £59-15 ($167.30). The Ministry of Food has also informed
the Board of its willingness to offer an incentive toward increased
production without invalidating the provisions of the present contract.
The amount of the incentive, its commencement date, and its duration
had not been established as of mid-February.

All copra exports and by-products from Fiji are bought and sold by
the Fiji Copra Board which was established by Fiji statutes. During
1951 the Board paid producers about 9 percent per ton less than the
Ministry of Food price in order to cover its costs of handling, insurance,
shrinkage, and administration.

An estimate of 1952 copra production cannot be made at present.
A particularly disastrous cyclone struck the Islands of Fiji on
January 29, 1952, and until a complete survey is made, the damage
caused the coconut groves remains unknown.

U.S. OLIVE OIL IMPORTS
DROP SHARPLY

United States imports of edible olive oil dropped sharply in 1951 to approximately one-half the 20-year high of 1950--from 39,644 to 20,208 short tons. Decreased purchases were the result, principally, of large stocks from the heavy buying of 1950.

Spain and Italy supplied 95 percent of the total arrivals with oil from Spain alone accounting for 68 percent. The relatively large shipments from Spain, in view of the small 1950 production, were made possible by record imports of United States soybean oil.

Inedible olive oil arrivals decreased also--from 4,382 tons in 1950 to 1,939 tons in 1951. Over 90 percent of the imports came from Portugal.

UNITED STATES: Edible olive oil imports, 1951 with comparisons
(Short tons)

Country of origin	Average 1935-39	1948	1949	1950 1/	1951 1/
Algeria..............	126	217	170	62	11
France..............	2,432	27	115	983	305
French Morocco........	3	4,786	1,042	133	-
Greece..............	2,452	892	36	29	20
Italy..............	15,766	8,319	4,752	12,207	5,518
Portugal..............	183	110	108	89	28
Spain..............	8,787	3,579	2,921	22,383	13,659
Syria and Lebanon.....	18	46	134	88	2/
Tunisia..............	1,600	-	446	3,597	546
Turkey..............	-	28	272	18	60
Other countries.......	38	47	28	55	61
Total........	31,405	18,051	10,024	39,644	20,208

UNITED STATES: Inedible olive oil imports, 1951 with comparisons
(Short tons)

Country of origin	Average 1935-39	1948	1949	1950 1/	1951 1/
Algeria..............	3,996	-	-	-	21
France..............	51	-	-	4	-
French Morocco........	37	62	22	37	44
Greece..............	5,505	2,322	14	50	-
Italy..............	1,868	2,436	1,422	181	-
Portugal..............	1,930	-	-	2,914	1,770
Spain..............	2,144	27	4	84	77
Syria and Lebanon.....	134	16	81	84	-
Tunisia..............	1,975	-	19	1,028	27
Turkey..............	37	22	-	-	-
Other countries.......	47	2	-	-	-
Total........	17,724	4,887	1,562	4,382	1,939

1/ Preliminary. 2/ Less than .5 ton
Compiled from official sources.

U.K. HERRING OIL OUTPUT
DOWN IN 1951

The United Kingdom's herring oil production in 1951 amounted to
2,800 short tons, a decrease of about 20 percent from the 3,520-ton
output of 1950, reports William Kling, Assistant Agricultural Attache,
American Embassy, London. Of the oil produced in 1951, 90 percent was
used for edible purposes, the remainder being diverted to non-edible
uses.

According to the Herring Industry Board of the United Kingdom,
the catch from the Scottish summer herring-fishing season was much
below expectation and the autumn East Anglican yield was less than
that of the previous year. The over-all reduction in the catch from
1950 of about 12,320 tons was felt most by the meal and oil reduction
factories. Herring diverted to these processing plants in 1951 amounted
to 30,240 tons, against 40,890 tons in 1950.

Prices of edible herring oil in 1951 averaged ₤128 per long ton
($320 per short ton). Oil sold for non-edible purposes averaged ₤95
($237.50) during the same period.

U.S. IMPORTS RECORD TONNAGE OF CASTOR
OIL, SMALLER QUANTITY OF BEANS

The United States imported a record volume--44,586 short tons--
of castor oil in 1951, compared with the previous high of 23,626 tons
in 1950 and only 113 tons prewar. Castor bean purchases of 74,558
tons were, however, the smallest since 1938, comparing with 113,114
tons in 1950 and the record high of 197,225 tons in 1941. Total
arrivals in bean equivalent amounted to 173,638 tons against 183,616
in 1950.

Oil imports from Brazil increased while bean imports decreased
although barter trade in castor and babassu oils was discontinued in
Brazil early in 1951. Over 78 percent of the oil, or a record 34,838
tons, and 68 percent of the beans--50,821 tons--originated in Brazil.
This, however, was the smallest volume of beans imported from that
country since 1935 and represented only about one-fourth the all-time
high of 194,370 tons received in 1941.

No castor beans were imported from India, at one time the
principal source of supply, from 1937 through 1939 and from 1944 until
1950. Following the 28,026-ton arrivals of 1950, imports dropped to
8,463 tons or roughly 10 percent of the 1951 total. Oil imports,
however, increased from only 294 tons in 1950 to 6,985 last year, in
accordance with India's policy of retaining seed supplies and pro-
moting oil exports.

The only other castor bean purchases of significant volume were
from Haiti and Ecuador.

UNITED STATES: Castor bean imports, 1951 with comparisons

(Short tons)

Country of origin	:Average :1935-39	1948	1949	1950 1/	1951 1/
North America:					
El Salvador............:	-	86:	114:	174:	283
Haiti..................:	133	2,896:	2,743:	3,148:	5,373
Other..................:	11	7:	15:	9:	137
Total..............:	144	2,989:	2,872:	3,331:	5,793
South America:					
Argentina.............:	269	-	-	-	-
Brazil................:	61,456	144,648:	137,912:	88,049:	50,821
Ecuador...............:	6	2,571:	2,319:	4,302:	4,307
Paraguay..............:	-	-	-	-	565
Total..............:	61,731	147,219:	140,231:	92,351:	55,693
Europe.................:	-	7:	1:	-	1
Asia:					
China.................:	112	-	-	1,253:	391
India.................:	1,960	-	-	28,026:	8,463
Other.................:	2,488	1,040:	1,395:	1,409:	2,826
Total..............:	4,560	1,040:	1,395:	30,688:	11,680
Africa................:	27	-	469:2/	4,744:	1,391
Grand total.......:	66,462	151,255:	144,968:	131,114:	74,558

UNITED STATES: Castor oil imports, 1951 with comparisons

(Short tons)

Country of origin	:Average :1935-39	1948	1949	1950 1/	1951 1/
North America...........:	-	-	10:	9:	31
South America:					
Argentina.............:	-	-	-	11:	104
Brazil................:	-	1,120:	5,273:3/	23,042:	34,838
Paraguay..............:	-	-	17:	103:	349
Peru..................:	-	-	-	-	44
Uruguay...............:	-	-	-	72:	55
Total..............:	-	1,120:	5,290:3/	23,228:	35,390
Europe.................:	71:	-	-	-	2,019
Asia:					
India.................:	-	-	-	294:	6,985
Thailand..............:	-	100:	9:	95:	-
Other.................:	42:	-	-	-	161
Total..............:	42:	100:	9:	389:	7,146
Grand total.......:	113:	1,220:	5,309:3/	23,626:	44,586

1/ Preliminary. 2/ Includes 4,523 tons from Angola. 3/ Revised.

Compiled from official sources.

U.S. TUNG OIL IMPORTS
DROP IN 1951

United States imports of tung oil in 1951 totaled only 14,853 short tons, a sharp decrease from the 56,242-ton arrivals in 1950, and only 24 percent as large as prewar. Imports from China, the chief source of supply prior to the Chinese embargo effective in mid-December 1950, dropped from 44,114 tons in that year to 5,590 tons. Arrivals from Argentina were somewhat less than in the 2 previous years but still made up almost half of the total 1951 importation. Smaller quantities were received from Brazil, Paraguay and Hong Kong.

UNITED STATES: Tung oil imports,
1951 with comparisons
(Short tons)

Country of origin	Average 1935-39	1948	1949	1950 1/	1951 1/
South America:					
Argentina................	-	-	8,244	9,306	7,199
Brazil..................	1	737	-	571	352
Paraguay................	-	-	66	302	861
Total.............	1	737	8,310	10,179	8,412
Europe.....................	126	-	-	-	2/
Asia:					
China...................	56,609	64,789	21,721	44,114	5,590
Hong Kong...............	4,725	1,081	2,453	1,949	851
Other...................	134	34			
Total.............	61,468	65,904	24,174	46,063	6,441
Grand total.........	61,595	66,641	32,484	56,242	14,853

1/ Preliminary. 2/ Less than .5 ton
Compiled from official sources.

INDIA'S FLAXSEED ACREAGE
DECREASES IN 1951-52

India's flaxseed acreage in 1951-52 has been placed at 2,535,000 acres, according to the first official estimate based on preliminary data, reports D. R. Gulati, American Embassy, New Delhi. This represents a decrease of 6.4 percent from the preceding year's corresponding estimate of 2,708,000 acres. Past experience indicates that the final estimate may be about 34 percent higher. The present first estimate is based on information available up to the middle of December 1951 and does not include the area under flaxseed sown with other crops, especially in the Uttar Pradesh.

Acreage decreases during the current year were reported by all of the flaxseed growing states except West Bengal, and were attributed primarily to unfavorable climatic conditions at sowing time. The general condition of the flaxseed crop as of mid-December 1951 was reported as satisfactory with the exception of that in certain parts of Bombay, Uttar Pradesh, and Hyderabad where conditions were below normal due to insufficient soil moisture.

COTTON AND OTHER FIBER

COTTON-PRICE QUOTATIONS
ON WORLD MARKETS

The following table shows certain cotton-price quotations on world markets converted at current rates of exchange.

COTTON: Spot prices in certain foreign markets, U.S. gulf-port average, and taxes incident to exports

Market location, kind, and quality	Date 1952	Unit of weight	Unit of currency	Price in foreign currency	Equiv. US¢ a lb. Spot quotation	Export & intermediate taxes
Alexandria		:Kantar				
Ashmouni, FG.........:	3-20	: 99.05 lbs.	:Tallari			
Ashmouni, Good......:	"	"	"			
Ashmouni, FGF.......:	"	"	"	Market closed		
Karnak, FG..........:	"	"	"			
Karnak, Good........:	"	"	"			
Karnak, FGF.........:	"	"	"			
Bombay		:Candy				
Jarila, Fine........:	"	: 784 lbs.	:Rupee	1/ 640.00	17.15	10.72
Broach Vijay, Fine..:	"	"	"	2/ 820.00	21.97	10.72
Karachi		:Maund				
4F Punjab, SG, Fine.:	3-18	: 82.28 lbs.	"	92.00	33.73	13.85
289F Sind, SG, Fine.:	"	"	"	(not available)		
289F Punjab, SG,Fine:	"	"	"	98.00	35.93	13.85
Buenos Aires		:Metric ton				
Type B............:	3-20	: 2204.6 lbs.	:Peso	8000.00	72.58	6.77
Lima		:Sp. quintal				
Tanguis, Type 3-1/2.:	"	: 101.4 lbs.	:Sol	(not quoted)		
Tanguis, Type 5.....:	"	"	"	(not quoted)		
Pima, Type 1........:	"	"	"	(not quoted)		
Recife		:Arroba				
Mata, Type 4........:	"	: 33.07 lbs.	:Cruzeiro	3/ 240.00	39.49	2.4% ad valorem
Sertao, Type 5......:	"	"	"	(not quoted)		" "
Sertao, Type 4......:	"	"	"	3/ 370.00	60.87	" "
Sao Paulo						
Sao Paulo, Type 5...:	"	"	"	285.00	46.89	3.0% ad valorem
Torreon		:Sp. quintal				
Middling, 15/16"....:	"	: 101.4 lbs.	:Peso	4/ 248.00	28.28	5.32
Houston-Galveston-New:						
Orleans av.Mid.15/16"	"	:Pound	:Cent	XXXXX	41.52	-----

Quotations of foreign markets and taxes reported by cable from U.S. Foreign Service posts abroad. U.S. quotations from designated spot markets.
1/ Reported 640.00 to 660.00 (17.68). Ceiling 820.00 (21.97).
2/ Reported 820.00 to 840.00 (22.50). Ceiling 925.00 (24.78).
3/ Nominal.
4/ Price received too late for inclusion in last week's table: Torreon, March 13. 1952, in pesos per Spanish quintal with U.S. cents per pound in parentheses, Middling, 15/16" 248.00 (28.28); taxes 5.32 U.S. cents.

OUTLOOK FOR PERUVIAN COTTON PRODUCTION
IN 1952 CONTINUES FAVORABLE

The prospects for the 1952-53 Pima cotton crop in Peru, to be picked
during July-September, have improved greatly in recent weeks, according
to Roy O. Westley, Agricultural Attache, American Embassy, Lima. A larger
supply of water for irrigation than was previously expected is reported
available in the northern Piura Valley where the bulk of the Pima crop is
grown. The improved supply of moisture will probably result in a substantial increase in acreage planted to this type of cotton in the Piura
Valley compared with the past 2 seasons when the water for irrigation was
more limited. The 1950-51 and 1951-52 Pima crops amounted to 27,000 and
29,000 bales (of 500 pounds gross), respectively, compared with the 67,000
bales harvested in 1949-50.

The outlook for the 1951-52 Tanguis cotton, with picking from April
through July, is also good. The area planted will probably be larger than
that of 1950-51 due to the favorable prices received by the growers from
last season's crop. More irrigated acreage has been made available through
extension of irrigation canals and installation of pumps for recovery of
ground water. Weather conditions have favored the development of the crop
thus far.

The sole unfavorable factor reported this season affecting the Tanguis
crop has been an outbreak of a cotton disease in several of the central
valleys. The disease, which has not been prevalent in Peru during recent
years, is a leaf fungus which practically defoliates the plant. While there
are adequate supplies of pesticides available in Peru to control normal
insect and disease damage, control of this particular fungus requires a
large quantity of sulphur which is in limited supply in the Western Hemisphere.
At present it is felt that the current outbreak can be effectively combatted,
but the drain on sulphur supplies may hamper the control of any future plagues
during the current season.

Despite this attack in several growing areas, production of Tanguis in
1951-52 may exceed the 340,000 bales produced in 1950-51 making a total crop
of at least 375,000 bales of all varieties.

U.S. COTTON EXPORTS
LOWER IN JANUARY

Exports of cotton from the United States in January 1952 amounted
to 700,000 bales of 500 pounds gross (676,000 running bales), making a
total for August-January 1951-52 of 3,674,000 bales (3,546,000 running
bales). This figure is about 63.5 percent above the total of 2,247,000
bales (2,149,000 running bales) for August-January 1950-51. The greatest
increases in the current season to date were in exports to India, the
United Kingdom, Belgium, and Spain.

The rapid decline in prices of foreign growths in recent weeks and
reports of prospective moderate reductions in mill consumption in a number
of the importing countries have caused some change in the outlook for
export trade in the remainder of the current season. However, United States
exports this season are still expected to reach or nearly reach 6 million
running bales. Export sales to date total approximately 5.2 million bales
(based on known sales, purchase programs, financing arrangements, and current
trade statistics).

UNITED STATES: Exports of cotton by countries of destination
averages 1934-38 and 1939-43; annual 1949-50 and 1950-51;
August-January 1950-51 and 1951-52

(Equivalent bales of 500 pounds gross)

Countries of destination	Year beginning August 1				August-January	
	Averages		1949-50	1950-51	1950-51	1951-52
	1934-38	1939-43				
	1,000 bales	1,000 bales	1,000 bales	1,000 bales	1,000 bales	1,000 bales
Austria................:	0:	1/ :	61:	55:	14:	14
Belgium-Luxembourg.....:	147:	43 :	192:	80:	48:	276
Czechoslovakia.........:	65:	0 :	58:	6:	6:	0
Denmark................:	35:	5 :	34:	31:	12:	24
Finland................:	35:	11 :	3:	3:	0:	16
France.................:	589:	154 :	794:	447:	232:	251
Germany................:	579:	4 :	759:	481:	224:	282
Greece.................:	2:	2 :	50:	1:	1:	0
Italy..................:	430:	12 :	749:	546:	166:	199
Netherlands............:	86:	34 :	259:	158:	68:	131
Norway.................:	13:	6 :	8:	20:	11:	13
Poland and Danzig......:	224:	1 :	47:	1:	1:	0
Spain..................:	101:	117 :	66:	66:	34:	166
Sweden.................:	93:	53 :	29:	33:	30:	73
Switzerland............:	2:	14 :	41:	22:	19:	94
United Kingdom.........:	1,097:	987 :	607:	307:	243:	503
Yugoslavia.............:	10:	7 :	26:	78:	24:	54
Other Europe...........: 2/	85:	146 : 3/	38:	12:	3:	17
Total Europe..........:	3,593:	1,596 :	3,821:	2,347:	1,136:	2,113
Canada.................:	261:	294 :	286:	431:	216:	185
Chile..................:	4/ :	5 :	39:	48:	10:	31
Colombia...............:	17:	9 :	63:	55:	28:	28
Cuba...................:	7:	11 :	19:	24:	15:	11
India..................:	44:	18 :	405:	219:	71:	474
China..................:	55:	106 :	132:	54:	54:	0
Japan..................:	1,271:	216 :	929:	883:	615:	680
French India and Indochina............:	4/ :	14 :	11:	16:	6:	11
Korea..................:	4/ :	n.a. :	52:	36:	14:	21
Australia..............:	5:	20 :	0:	0:	0:	42
Other countries.......:	43:	7 : 5/	247:	167:	82:	78
Total...............:	5,296:	2,296 :	6,004:	4,280:	2,247:	3,674

1/ Included with Germany.　2/ Includes 39 Portugal, 23 Soviet Union.　3/ Includes
24 Hungary, 5 Rumania.　4/ If any, included in Other Countries.　5/ Includes
144 Hong Kong, 41 Manchuria.

Compiled from official records of the Bureau of the Census.

LIVESTOCK AND ANIMAL PRODUCTS

WOOL SITUATION
IN URUGUAY

The 1951-52 Uruguayan wool clip is now estimated at about 185 million pounds, greasy basis, according to Camara Mercantil de Productor del Pais, as reported by Dale E. Farringer, Agricultural Attache, American Embassy, Montevideo. Because of overgrazing and less food available per animal as a result of over-stocking; dealers complain that this season's clip is lighter in weight and of shorter fiber length. Furthermore, the percentage of coarser wool (below 60's) is higher today than in previous years because of the practice of ranchers to increase Corriedale flocks and breed fewer crosses such as Merino-Lincoln and Merino-Romney Marsh. According to one large Uruguayan exporter only 27 percent of the 1951-52 clip will average 60's or better, now in demand in the Boston market.

Wool sale continues slow. During the first 4 months (October-January) not more than 1.5 million pounds of the 1951-52 clip had moved into export sales channels. Wool deliveries have been sizeable and about 30 percent of the clip is in storage at Montevideo. Exports of tops, and yarn, which are of larger volume than raw wool exports have been derived from the carry-over.

Final accounting of the 1950-51 clip indicates that about 133 million pounds were exported as greasy or washed wool; 23 million pounds were processed for export; about 12 million pounds were consumed locally and about 18 million pounds were carried over on September 30, 1951. At the end of January nearly 8 million pounds of the 1950-51 clip and 176 million pounds of the 1951-52 clip appeared to be on hand in Uruguay.

BRADFORD CARPET WOOL
EXPORTS TO U. S. HEAVY

Heavy shipments of carpet wool continue to be made from Bradford to the United States. Total shipments of wool and hair for the months of February 1952 at 1.2 million pounds were the largest for any month since August 1950. Most of the wool exported has been Scotch Blackface, Welsh mountain fleece and other carpet types produced in the British Isles while some has been of East Indian origin.

Another feature of Bradford exports to the United States in February has been the preponderance of woolen cloth over worsted cloth. The 126,737 square yards of cloth exported in the week ended February 29 included 81,019 square yards of woolen cloth and 45,718 square yards of worsted cloth. This was the fourth week in which exports of woolen cloth greatly exceeded those of worsted.

Total exports of cloth to the United States in February 1952 amounted to over 530,000 square yards compared with just slightly over 500,000 square yards in February 1951.

GRAINS, GRAIN PRODUCTS AND FEEDS

BURMA EXPORTS LESS
RICE IN JANUARY

Burma's rice exports of 142 million pounds in January were smaller
than 190 million pounds during the corresponding month of 1952. The
comparatively low trade resulted from low year-end stocks and the lack
of contracts between Burma and the buyer nations for the sale of rice.
Shipments to countries of destination were as follows (million pounds):
India, 33; United Kingdom, 26; Ceylon, 25; Malaya, 16; Japan, 14;
Mauritius, 14; Persian Gulf, 11; British Borneo, 2; and other countries, 1.

CANADA'S RICE
IMPORTS INCREASE

Canada's 1951 rice imports in terms of milled totaled 79 million
pounds compared with 60 million pounds during a year earlier. A
feature of the year's trade was a shift from the importation of rough
rice toward imports classified in the official trade statistics as
cleaned rice. This classification apparently includes brown rice.

Canada: Rice imports, by country of origin,
average 1936-40, annual 1947-51

Country of origin	Average 1936-40	1947	1948	1949	1950	1951
	Million pounds	Million pounds	Million pounds	Million pounds	Million pounds	Million pounds
Uncleaned 1/						
United States...:	11.8	54.1	59.7	50.1	52.8	33.9
India and Burma.:	25.4	0	0	0	0	0
Hong Kong.......:	5.2	0	0	0	0	0
Japan..........:	5.8	0	0	0	0	0
Thailand.......:	4.3	0	0	0	13.1	0
Egypt..........:	1.2	0	0	0	9.9	4.2
Brazil.........:	1.9	0	0	0	8.8	2.1
Other countries.:	1.4	0	0	0	0	0.7
Total	57.0	54.1	59.7	50.1	84.6	40.9
Cleaned						
United States...:	5.5	3.3	0.5	0.6	4.9	10.9
Brazil.........:	0	0	0	0	0	33.0
Other countries.:2/	8.4	0	0	0	0 :3/	7.8
Total.......:	13.9	3.3	0.5	0.6	4.9	51.7

1/ Uncleaned, unhulled, paddy. 2/ Includes 6.0 million pounds from
Hong Kong. 3/ Includes 4.1 million pounds from Thailand and 3.5 million
from Netherlands.

Trade of Canada.

The principal sources for 1951 imports were Brazil and the United States. Imports of rice classified as cleaned from Brazil increased sharply, while imports of rough rice declined from the United States. Other countries of origin were Egypt, Thailand, and the Netherlands.

(Continued on next page)

D A I R Y P R O D U C T S--(Continued from Page 238)

the drought was broken in late February and conditions are expected to improve. Australia has experienced a very unsatisfactory summer season to date. Although some of the drought-stricken areas have recently received beneficial rains, no substantial increase in milk production is expected until late this year, since many cows have dried off and others are far advanced in their lactation period. In Argentina, pastures are deteriorating because of insufficient rains.

In Western Europe, the incidence of foot-and-mouth disease appears to be under control. The recent downward trend in cow numbers in Denmark which was aggravated by the presence of this disease at the end of the year, suggests that in 1952 production of milk and milk products may be a little less than in 1951. Output in Sweden in the current year is expected to be somewhat lower than that of last year, due to above-normal slaughter, reduced use of commercial feed because of high prices, and below-normal supply of hay.

Feed supplies in the United Kingdom are generally satisfactory, the winter so far has been mild, and there has been ample roughage with adequate supplies of rationed concentrates. Dairy animals are generally reported to be in very good condition. However, the government controlled milk prices are not considered adequate to encourage any increase in milk cow numbers.

In Canada, farms are well supplied with home-grown feed, and the increased volume of hay caused a slight price reduction from last year. However, this favorable situation has been partially offset by increased prices for mill-feeds and protein supplements. Milk production in the United States probably will be somewhat smaller than in 1951. Fluid milk consumption is expected to expand still further, resulting in lower supplies being available for product manufacture.

Annual:

The year 1951 as a whole was not favorable for the output of factory dairy products in the countries for which data are available 1/ and over-all output was less than in 1950. Total butter production was down 6 percent, despite sizable increases in Western Germany, Switzerland, the Union of South Africa and New Zealand. Total cheese output was down 2 percent although there were significant increases in Denmark, the Netherlands, and Sweden. Total output of canned milk in 1951 was just under that of 1950 with increases in Canada and the Netherlands almost offsetting the decreased production in the United States and the United Kingdom. Total dried milk output was down 15 percent from the level of 1950 with major decreases occurring in the United States, the Netherlands, and the United Kingdom.--By Regina M. Murray, based in part upon U. S. Foreign Service repo

1/ (See table on Page 239)

GRAINS, GRAIN PRODUCTS AND FEEDS--(Continued from preceding page)

UNION OF SOUTH AFRICA
EXPECTS SMALL CORN CROP

The 1951-52 corn crop in the Union of South Africa is expected to
be somewhat below normal domestic requirements, according to the American
Embassy at Pretoria. The present outlook for the corn crop is considered
serious since corn is the primary food of the native population as well
as important to the livestock industry.

Early-season reports were quite optimistic, with some prospects of
another large crop such as the near-record harvests of the past 2 seasons.
Latest information, however, takes account of serious drought damage and
forecasts a crop of less than 60 million bushels. This is short of domestic
requirements of about 85 million bushels even with the expected carry-over
stocks of 18-20 million bushels.

The drought, which started in late October, is described as the worst
since 1932-33. Except for sporadic showers, no relief had been received
at latest report. The corn harvest normally takes place in April/May.
A substantial part of the crop is considered beyond relief even if rains
were received. However, some of the late-planted corn could benefit
from rains.

The earlier harvested winter grains were not affected by the drought.
On the contrary, dry conditions at harvest time were beneficial, and the
wheat outturn was the second largest of record. Barley was also a good
crop with an increase of 30 percent over the previous harvest. The
quality of the grain is good and some exportable surplus of barley is
expected. Production of oats was about 25 percent less than the previous
crop. The reduction was attributed to damage from unseasonable wind
storms in November.

The controlled prices of both corn and wheat are expected to be
increased for the 1952-53 season. The Government will need to raise
the price paid corn producers to maintain corn acreage at the required
level, since competition from other crops such as wheat, has in some
cases reduced the corn acreage. An increase is also expected for
wheat, since production costs for all grains have risen sharply in the
past 2 seasons.

Prices to producers for bagged corn of the better grades during the
1951-52 marketing season were the equivalent of $1.04 per bushel in
United States currency. That price was about 10 cents per bushel more
than the price paid for the crop of the previous year.

The Control Boards for winter grains and corn have exclusive
authority for the purchase and sales of these grains. Imports and exports
are also controlled by the Boards.

The Government is continuing to subsidize the price to consumers.
Corn is sold to consumers at 4 cents per bushel less than the price the
government pays to producers. An additional part of the subsidy is
made available for defraying the cost of handling, storage and marketing.

LATE NEWS

(Continued from Page 233)

in 1951-52. Recent imports of 4,00 bales from the United States, combined with this enlarged production, the official went on to say, will make it unnecessary for the country to import additional cotton in 1952 or 1953.

- - - -

The final official estimate of the 1951-52 cotton crop in Burma placed production at 32,200 bales (of 500 pounds gross), somewhat below the 35,000 bales harvested in 1950-51. However, this estimate covers only the wagaletype cotton, excluding a small production of wagyi cotton which will be reported at a later date.

- - - -

The Government of Italy recently concluded trade agreements with Iraq and Iran, both of which provide for imports of raw cotton, among other items. The agreement with Iraq provides for about 9,200 bales of cotton (of 500 pounds gross) to be imported into Italy during the 1-year period beginning March 1, 1952. Under the Iranian agreement Italy will receive up to $1,400,000 worth of cotton during the 12-month period beginning February 3, 1952. At current prices this would amount to about 5,500 bales of cotton.

- - - -

Egyptian cotton prices will be supported by the government (announcement March 17) at 125 tallaris per cantar (72.25 cents) for Karnak, Good - July futures and 72 tallaris (41.62 cents) for Ashmouni, Good - August futures. Both prices are below the current market level.

Lightning Source UK Ltd.
Milton Keynes UK
UKHW021006161218
334046UK00008B/799/P